# HOW M  T!

**Compiled by**

**Will Hanafin**

**and**
**Ray D'Arcy**
**Jenny Kelly**
**Mairéad Farrell**

*The Ray D'Arcy Show*

MENTOR
BOOKS

First Published in 2005 by

MENTOR BOOKS
43 Furze Road,
Sandyford Industrial Estate,
Dublin 18,
Republic of Ireland.

Tel: + 353 1 295 2112 / 3    Fax: + 353 1 295 2114
e-mail: admin@mentorbooks.ie
www.mentorbooks.ie

The views and opinions expressed in this book are entirely those of
the contributors and do not necessarily reflect the views of the
publisher. The publishers do not accept any responsibility for any
loss or damage suffered by any person as a result of the information
provided in this book.

ISBN 1-84210-329-6

A catalogue record for this book
is available from the British Library

Text Inputting: Design & Layout: Nicola Sedgwick

Printed in Ireland by ColourBooks Ltd.
1 3 5 7 9 10 8 6 4 2

# Foreword

This is a work of non-fiction, although reading most of the testimonies and newspaper clippings herein you would be forgiven for thinking otherwise. Some of the tales read like the work of creative and sometimes demented minds – stories conceived in people's wild imaginations with no connection to the real world. But, folks, fact is indeed stranger than fiction. We have unearthed a rich vein of unbelievable true stories. They are proof if such is needed that we live in not a small but a tiny world, and that the strangest things can happen in the company of children and animals.

For those who are unfamiliar with our radio programme, the 'Bobblehead Ray' is a much sought after and very silly-looking figurine which is given exclusively to listeners who wow, amuse and entertain us with their *How Mad Is That!* stories. We have complemented our listeners' experiences with those mad stories from the daily newspapers that make you question the sanity of the world in which we live.

Finally the thank yous bit – Thank you to Jenny Kelly and Mairead Farrell, our 'Arbiters of Madness' and special thanks to our head compiler Will Hanafin. Go raibh maith agat to Nicola and Claire at Mentor and to the Boss-men Willie and Danny. Finally thanks to Denise Conway who gave birth to Bobblehead Ray, and to our funny and generous listeners who live mad lives – well, sometimes anyway! Thank you, thank you, thank you, enjoy.

*Ray D'Arcy*

# **Contents**

# When the nibbles strike

I was shearing sheep one day wearing a vest top. I was shearing around the sheep's tail when suddenly I gave out a big scream like a little girl. The sheep was nibbling on the hair under my arm. I had a little bald patch there when I checked in the mirror that evening.

*How mad is that!*
Dave, Kerry

# Watt A dOg

We have a sheepdog at home called Buddy who has a fondness for lightbulbs. He likes to chew glass into small pieces, leaving just the metal, but never swallows anything. He has got through eight bulbs in one day including a few 150 watts. He's had a few X-rays and he's grand. Fortunately our recycling glass is now on a shelf.

*How mad is that!*
Rich, Kildare

## FIELD SNAKE

My sister was taking a break from studying for her Leaving Cert and went for a walk in the fresh air. She was walking through a nearby field when she spotted one of our neighbours. He appeared to have something in his hands. As she got closer she could see he was playing with a snake – or as he said 'exercising it'. He proceeded to give her a lecture as to how dangerous the snake was, and then asked her if she'd like to hold it!

*How mad is that!*
Jenny, Wicklow

# NEWSPAPER MADS...

## False Start

A disgruntled punter was suspected of involvement after 15 Galway bookies were locked out of their premises because their doors were superglued during the annual racing festival.

The bookmakers had to smash windows to gain entry during their busiest week of the year.

## Special Branch

A conservationist put a one-metre branch from one of the felled O'Connell Street trees on the auction site eBay. Brian Keegan, a trainee accountant, placed a €10 reserve on the branch of the plane tree.

He says any money raised will be donated to Greenpeace, and says the branch cannot be posted because of its awkward length.

# NEWSPAPER MADS...

## Fishwife

A man was convicted of common assault after hitting his wife over the head with an 4kg dead pike.

He came home from the pub with the fish with the intention of cooking it, but became involved in a bust up with his wife instead.

'I was totally wrong. I had a few and can just remember dangling the pike over her head. I cooked it for the cats in the end.'

## Head Wrecker

An Englishman was jailed for five and a half months for tearing the head off his pet parrot.

The judge said, 'You might be described as Wolverhampton's Ozzy Osbourne.'

# Third Time Lucky

THE MOST WONDERFUL thing happened to me a while ago. I was at a table quiz and we lost. We realised quite early that we hadn't a hope of winning and set our sights on the loser's booby prize instead.

But we couldn't even get that right and came joint losers. There was a tie breaker, and we lost.

Then came the raffle. We had tickets 101 to 109 and the first prize was Number 100. We lost again.

The winners of the raffle were sitting next to us. They had got loads of goodies, brilliant prizes and they didn't even know that the greatest prize they got was not the tickets or CDs or gadgets. They had a Bobblehead Ray!

I sweet-talked them into giving him to me. My night was complete and I drove home glowing with happiness. I lost three times and came out a winner.

*How mad is that!*
Nicki, Meath

# NEWSPAPER MADS...

## In the Pink

A couple got a shock when their white cat turned pink during a morning stroll.

Philip and Joan Worth have been told by vets that Brumas has not been poisoned. But no explanation can be found for the Barbie Pink rinse he has developed after walking near his home.

# NEWSPAPER MADS...

# Spud Ugly

Irish supermarkets have come up with the idea of a 'value pack,' containing vegetables that aren't good looking enough to be sold singly.

Class 1 produce include glossy apples, perfectly orange carrots and waxy skinned potatoes.

Lowly Class 2 produce are nutritionally as good but are not endowed with the same good looks as the Class 1 variety.

# G'Day!

Ray, I was once swimming on Bondi Beach in Australia and a penguin swam past me.
*How mad is that!*
Abi

# ReSuRrEcTiOn

My dad put my sister's hamster in a box in the ground because he said he was dead. The next morning my dad went to the garage to get something and found the hamster had dug his way out of the box and went back into the garage. He was still alive.
*How mad is that!*

18

# *Ferret Laughs*

I was in Kilkenny for the Cat Laughs Festival recently. After an amazing Saturday night out my friends and myself were walking home when we saw an albino ferret. I kid you not. He was just strolling up the street minding his own business.

*How mad is that!*
Sean White

# UnLuCkY

I was on my first date with this girl, who owned a horse. As I'd never been on a horse before she promised she'd let me ride hers. I thought this would be a pretty good deal. Within a few minutes of being in the saddle, the horse freaked out and went into a full gallop. I was dismounted but my foot was caught in the stirrup and I was dragged for 200 yards.

She managed to stop the horse, but when I got to my feet I was in a great deal of pain. She convinced me to breathe into the horse's nostrils to calm it down. Suddenly it threw its head into the air sharply catching me under the chin. It knocked me out cold. She called an ambulance while I was unconscious. I woke in the ambulance to hear the paramedics say, 'I think we'll have to cut this off.' I was a bit perturbed, but it turned out it was my sleeve – I had shattered my elbow.

*How mad is that!*

Pete Andow

# BOXING CLEVER

The other day I was stopped at a set of traffic lights and I noticed a boxer dog sitting at the junction. When the green man came up on the light opposite him he calmly got up and crossed the road.

*How mad is that!*
Pearse, Louth

## Rats

I nearly killed my fiancé at the weekend coming home from the pub. We were in Dublin walking, holding hands, when suddenly I saw a rat, which I'm really scared of. In my panic I pushed my fiancé out in front of a taxi to get away from the rat.

*How mad is that!*
Teresa

# BaCk FrOm ThE dEaD

A person my friend knows found his dog dragging next-door's rabbit around the back garden – dead.

The neighbours were out so he chanced a lightning run to the pet shop, matched the rabbit's colour and markings as best he could, then snuck the replacement back into the neighbour's back garden.

When the neighbour's kids returned he was listening out to make sure he'd successfully made the switch. There were screams of terror from next door. He was mistaken because it wasn't actually the neighbour's rabbit the dog had snatched – their rabbit had died a few weeks previously.

*How mad is that!*
Paul

# It was this big!

A while ago I was fishing in Maynooth on a nice sunny day near the train station on the Royal Canal. All day I was there without even a bite when suddenly my float shot down beneath the water with such speed that I thought, 'This must be a big one.' I then started to reel in but it didn't feel like the average roach or perch. So whilst I was reeling in I noticed something going berserk on the far riverbank beside the train station.

Then it occurred to me that indeed I had hooked a duck! So during the madness of me trying to get the duck in, so I could try to remove the hook and line, a train load of people walked out into the car park where all these old women started shouting abuse at me, thinking I was doing this intentionally. Within minutes two policemen had arrived from the local police station, which the old ladies must have called! I nearly got arrested for poaching!

*How mad is that!*

Cheers, Tony

# HOLEY UNACCEPTABLE

I lived in Middlesex in England in the mid 90s and myself and my wife rented a top flat in an old three storey house in Harrow. After a couple of months my brother-in-law came to stay. We had a small dormer windowsill and used to get visits from a squirrel that lived in the trees out the back garden. He would peek through the window as we all watched TV.

We took to feeding the squirrel in the mornings, and named him 'Hairy Hole'.

We loved watching him wrestle with the bag of nuts. So much so that we went to a pet shop and asked for ladders and mini assault equipment for small animals as we wanted Hairy Hole to work a bit harder to get the food. She said she would report us for animal cruelty.

It got worse. All the flats in the house had intercoms on the front door. One morning a neighbour heard my brother-in-law shout, 'Did you feed Hairy Hole?' I was so embarrassed and could not look this person in the eye again.

*How mad is that!*
Colin

# *Free Ride*

I was going into town on top of a double decker bus, when suddenly I heard a thump and saw something fly past the window. I looked up and what did I see? At the front of the bus, stuck on the window, was a pigeon's arse, wings still flapping.

What must have happened was two pigeons flying side by side in the middle of the road at around the same speed as the bus when the bus caught up with them. The pigeon slowly slid off and flew past the window to join its friend, while I desperately tried not to laugh out loud in front of the many Japanese tourists sitting at the front, looking quite bewildered.

*How mad is that!*
Lara Walsh

# FiShY sMell

One evening after a hard day's fishing my dad collected me and a friend and was dropping my friend home. When I was taking his gear out of the boot I must have knocked over a tub of maggots. However I didn't take my gear out until the next day so it was only then I noticed the empty tub. I didn't know where they went. My dad found out weeks after when every two minutes he had to roll down his car window to let loads of blue bottles out! In the morning sometimes there would be about 60 buzzing inside the car, and he was a taxi man.

*How mad is that!*

Tony

# BACK SEAT DRIVER

My dog Colleen is a West Highland terrier and very smart.

Sometimes when I stop at the local newsagents for the morning paper I get detained because the girl in the shop is very talkative. When this happens Colleen jumps behind the wheel and presses the horn – beeping like mad until I come out.

*How mad is that!*
Brian Lochrai

# In-Car Entertainment

I'M NOT A TAXI DRIVER but I do work in a pub down the country and often end up taxiing drunken people home. I really need a Bobblehead Ray. The drunken people would talk to you, play with you all the way home and dream about you in their drunken  coma sleeps. Your best fans are waiting patiently for Bobblehead Ray.

*How mad is that!*

Mary and Joanne

# NEWSPAPER MADS...

## Long Story!

An infestation of daddy long legs has forced the closure of a racecourse.

Chepstow racecourse has cancelled races for two weeks after a jockey suffered back injuries and his horse had to be destroyed after a fall. The incident was linked to a weakening of the turf on the course caused by an infestation of daddy long legs. They feed on grass roots.

## Long Story!

Council officials in Clare have issued a warning to bathers not to swim with a dolphin living off the coast. It comes after a 41-year-old German tourist was hospitalised with abdominal injuries after being rammed by the dolphin.

A number of incidents have been reported in connection with the dolphin including butting people in the ribs and face, or pinning them to the seabed for long periods.

**NEWSPAPER MADS...**

# Quackers

It's not just the politicians that are an endangered species in Leinster House.

Animal welfare officials had to be brought into the Dáil recently because so many members of a family of ducks that had taken up residence in the pond had died.

One senator quipped when he heard three of the fowl had died that, 'We certainly don't want any dead ducks around the Houses of the Oireachtas.'

# Birdbrained

I'm a student in Limerick and one day my roomie told me that a bird keeps flying into her window repeatedly every morning and waking her up. Obviously I broke down laughing and really thought she had lost it this time, until later that evening I decided to tell the lads I live with the story she had come up with. To my astonishment one of them said he had seen it too, one morning when he was brushing his teeth in the bathroom, and the bird scared the living daylights out of him.

I still couldn't believe it so about a week later I was in the kitchen having my breakfast when I heard a weird banging noise upstairs. I ran to the bottom of the stairs and saw the shadow of a bird hitting against the window. I was amazed.

Since then I have heard it on several occasions and it still happens.

Also I think I know what it looks like – as I couldn't see through the bathroom window because it's frosted. One morning while getting breakfast again I heard the bird but then it stopped and flew to the tree at the end of the garden. It was small enough, but really old and battered and had the biggest belly I have ever seen.

*How mad is that!*
Karen

# Smoke Alarm

The Ray D'Arcy Show
**WINNER**

WE WERE WOKEN today to the smell of smoke in the house. Last night my dad decided to start cooking the meat for today's dinner, except he put it on and forgot to turn it off. My sister got up first and saw our beautiful golden Labrador Ben in the kitchen gasping for life. There were tears rolling down his face and he raced for the door as soon as she opened it.

I turned off the cooker and moved the now empty pot off the ring. When I put the pot in the sink and filled it with water to cool it down, the arse fell off. My mother then got up and blew a gasket as the walls of the kitchen were only painted last Saturday.

Eventually my dad decided to get up and face the music. He joked that he had told the rest of us to turn off the meat.

All day long when I went to work I could smell soot off me. I am beginning to think it's my hair. Just before lunch I got a call from my mother to say that Ben the dog had taken a turn for the worse and had to go to the vet for smoke inhalation. The vet treated him for shock as he was still shivering six hours after the event.

*How mad is that!*
Muiriosa Ryan

# Prince Charming

I was out in Cork on Tuesday night and I found a girl's white shoe. I left early with the shoe in hand and went home to a party. It was all good until I explained it to a girl I kind of knew next door and it turned out to be hers. She showed me her other shoe.

She was my Cinderella.

*How mad is that!*

John, Cork

# Hair Apparent

I hated hairy-backed men all my life. My friend and myself used to laugh at them on beaches. Now I'm engaged to one and when I'm in bed the hair goes up my nose. But I love him so much I don't care. I keep it a secret from my friend though.

*How mad is that!*

39

# TRUE LOVE

When I first met my fiancé he was working in a shop and we spent many blissful weeks of me buying things and him selling and us flirting and all the usual stuff that goes with two people being attracted to each other.

Then one day I said to myself enough is enough, I have to at least find out this guy's name. In a flash of inspiration I decided to do something that I would need to be sponsored for, ask him to sponsor me and in turn get his name and address. So I put myself through a 24 hour Trocaire fast just to get to know him a little better.

What I didn't realise was that while I was in the shop one day weeks before the 'fast' idea struck, I had completed a lotto slip for a local GAA team and handed it to the cashier. My fiancé saw me and had a good old nose when I left so he actually knew my name and address well before I knew his. If I had known this, would I have put myself through the fast . . . not so sure!

These events only emerged when we eventually started dating two and a half years later. We recently got engaged and are buying our first home together.

*How mad is that!*
Mairead, Dublin

# NEWSPAPER MADS...

## Love Hurts... Your Pocket

The average person spends more than €55,000 trying to find love during their lifetime.

During the first six months of a relationship men spend an average of €2,000 on their partner, nearly double that spent by women at €740.

But once the relationship goes past the 12 month barrier men's spending drops off!

# Decent Proposal

I'M GOING TO Canada soon with my girlfriend of two years. I plan on proposing to her in Niagara, corny I know but that's half the fun of it. I wanted to bring a Bobblehead Ray with me and hang the engagement ring around his neck and put it on the dinner table while I'm proposing to her. She loves your show and  is gutted that when she moved jobs she couldn't listen to your show anymore.

Please can I have a Bobblehead Ray. We'll send photos of our trip with Bobblehead Ray from the glass floor of the CN tower in Toronto, and in Niagara.

*How mad is that!*

Dave

# *Crossed Wires*

My ex once asked me what '*Tu sais*' means in English. I told him 'You know.' after repeating this between us in a confusing way a few times, he got cross, saying, 'If I knew I wouldn't keep asking.'

Another time we were talking about making bread as part of his cooking course and I said, you have to 'prove it'. (That's a special chamber that you put bread in to let it rise.) He replied that 'having the bread was proof enough'.

*How mad is that!*
Claire

# DrEaM lOVEr

Last night I dreamt my boyfriend surprised me at work with a trip to Paris. I was so excited as we went to the airport. Would he finally show me how much he loved me and produce the sought after gift to prove this?

We got to Paris and the next thing we were on the Eiffel tower having dinner. I was almost drunk with excitement.

After the main course he got down on one knee and put his hand in his pocket. He pulled out a small box with a diamond ring in it. I was heartbroken and stormed off in a huff. I thought he was going to give me my most sought after Bobblehead Ray. And he thought he was going to snag himself a wife!

*How mad is that!*

Triona, Cork

PS: If I don't receive a Bobblehead Ray I may just never marry.

# Tea for Two

The Ray D'Arcy Show

**WINNER**

I WAS IN A CAFÉ earlier and a girl was sitting diagonal to me at the same table and *Today FM* was playing and I noticed she drank her tea the exact same as me, really milky with one sugar, as we were both listening to you.

I said jokingly, 'Look at that, looks like we could have the perfect relationsip.'

After a lot of joking and flirting the time to go came, and we swapped numbers for the laugh. We have been texting non-stop since. So cheers team.

*How mad is that!*

# NEWSPAPER MADS...

## Dub Snub

A woman driver in her car is more likely to be aided by kind hearted rural drivers than by Dublin motorists.

In Dublin only one in 70 passing vehicles will stop to help a woman driver if she's changing a wheel on the road.

## You Old Romantics!

Sacre bleu! It's been revealed that Irish men are more romantic than French guys. The Irish male scored highly in the international survey of 10,000 men, coming sixth out of 37 countries.

True romantic Irish blokes came up trumps when they said they prefer romance to wealth.

# Some Holiday!

A girl in the office is planning to get married in September. They bought a house last year and have been saving for the wedding so money has been tight. On top of that the guy has spent the last six months doing peace-keeping somewhere in Africa.

When he came home they decided to push the boat out and went to Portugal for a week.

On their first day they were lying on the beach when some guy robbed their bag containing money, an MP3 player, her glasses and other bits and pieces. They spent the next two days filing police reports and trying to make the best of their holiday.

On the Wednesday night she was going to the loo when she passed out and crashed on the floor smacking her head and splitting her elbow. She had to go to the doctor who then sent her to the hospital for X-rays and stitches.

*How mad is that!*

Martin

# POLES APART

Myself and a friend were sitting on a bus waiting to cross into Argentina from Brazil. A French guy and an Israeli girl were chatting to each other on the bus as we waited for the bus driver to return with our passports from border control.

When the passports came back the same two people began to compare passports. The girl says to the guy that he looks like her brother. Then they realise they have the same surname – a very rare Polish one. It turns out that these two people have the same grandfather who fled Poland during the war and whose children got separated. One ended up in Israel and the other in France. This made a couple of random strangers on a bus first cousins!

*How mad is that!*

Gracie Leonard

# *Wherever I Lay My Hat . . .*

Last September I went to the Oktoberfest in Munich with four Aussie guys who were working over here for a year. While we were sitting drinking our Stein and singing in the Hofbrau tent, one of the guys spotted a girl wearing a brown beanie cap. He said he used to have a hat just like that, but he lost it about a year ago when he left it at a house party in Brisbane before he moved up here. After a few more drinks he went to chat to the girl wearing the hat, and she turned out to be an Aussie from Brisbane who found the hat cleaning up after a house party in Brisbane a year previous. So my mate Luke got his hat back, half the world away from where he lost it.

*How mad is that!*
Brian Condron

# CROWE ABOUT THIS

Last year while living in Sydney my housemates and I discovered that Russell Crowe owned an apartment fairly close to where we were staying. We thought this was pretty exciting in itself, and never thought we'd meet him. Then one night while we were watching *Gladiator* we got a call from a friend to say we could see 'him' in the flesh if we went down to the local. There he was, sitting at the bar with a load of his mates. We got one photo with him, he bought us all a round of drinks and then when we were kicked out of the pub he came back to our house and stayed for a couple of hours. We were on such a buzz we didn't sleep for days and the only words we could utter were, 'Russell Crowe was in our house.'

*How mad is that!*
Jackie, Kildare

# REMEMBER ME?

Last year I was coming back from Thailand via Amsterdam. I was on the flight back from Amsterdam to Dublin and I left the stub off my boarding pass in the magazine holder of my seat. Nothing mad about that, but a girl that I used to work with was coming back from a year in Oz a couple of weeks later and she pulled out a magazine from the holder in front of her seat and guess what fell out? My boarding pass! What are the chances!

*How mad is that!*
Barry

# Window Dressing

I WAS ATTENDING a friend's wedding last year and was dressed very elegantly, wearing a long black tight strapless dress. We had to travel just over one hour to the hotel, so when we got out of the car I decided to straighten myself up.

Looking in what I thought was a mirror I reached into my boob tube and repositioned myself one side at a time only to realise it wasn't a mirror but the window into the restaurant.

*How mad is that!*

# NEWSPAPER MADS...

## Invasion of the Giant...Rhubarb?

Residents in Achill Island are worried that their island is being taken over by giant rhubarb.

The plant can grow up to three metres long and is slowly taking over fields. Local politicians now want a study carried out to see what can kill it, as it's immune to most pesticides.

# NEWSPAPER MADS...

## Wings Clipped!

Racing pigeons have been banned from racing on Ireland's East Coast because they keep colliding with aircraft.

The Irish Homing Union announced races are now to begin in Tramore.

There were fears of a plane crash after a flock of 21,000 pigeons crashed into a plane taking off at Dublin, which was then forced to make an emergency landing.

# NEWSPAPER MADS...

## *Woof! I'm on the Train!*

An impatient dog called Archie caught the train home on his own after becoming separated from his owner.

The black Labrador boarded the Scotrail train from Aberdeen to Inverness.

Owner Mike Taitt thought his dog was lost until he received a phone call saying Archie got off the train only three miles from his home.

# Cold Case

My wife and son were flying to London for a week's holidays. Because I couldn't take time off work to take them to the airport I thought the Aircoach was the best option. My missus wasn't keen but I told her it would be fine and she finally agreed. When she got to the airport she realised somebody had taken her case and left in its place a smaller, tattier version. She told the driver, who shrugged his shoulders. She ran around the airport to see if she could see her case. She told someone at the information desk, who informed the Gardai. They opened the tatty case to see if there was a phone number or contact name inside. They found a number but it was out of use. My wife and son decided to travel anyway.

Finally the Gardai traced the bag – the person who took her bag had travelled to Paris. The airline my wife flew with didn't fly from Paris to London, so the bag had to be sent to Manchester. From Manchester it was to be flown to London.

She was told she would have the bag that evening. Then it was 48 hours later. Then they said they lost the bag. Then they said they thought it was in Manchester. Then we heard Manchester never received it. Then we were told to wait another two weeks – and finally we were informed it was officially lost.

All this time my wife was ringing all three airports: Dublin, Manchester and London.

Just when we had written the whole thing off we got a call from Dublin airport and guess what, the case never left Dublin.

*How mad is that!*
Tim Kavanagh

# Oh Boy - Danny

Just under a year ago my friend and I were living in Sydney. We were packing because we were heading around Oz the following day. Around midnight when we'd finished packing we said we'd head into the city for a pint, as you do. Before we went into the pub we had to go to the shop first. We were queuing for the ATM when we heard a middle-aged Irish woman at the counter asking for a phone card so she could call home.

She was having a bit of trouble so my friend went up to her and helped her buy the right phone card and explained how she would use it. She was with two guys and they were all really grateful to us for helping them.

Half an hour or so later we bumped into two lads in a nightclub. They were Irish and said they were touring with Daniel O'Donnell. We didn't believe them and so they pointed over to a corner and there was Daniel.

He headed over to us accompanied by the two guys who were with the lady in the shop.

'These are the two lovely girls who helped Josephine in the shop,' said one of them.

'Josephine has been my friend and mentor for 15 years,' said Daniel.

From that we went to on to hang around with Daniel and his posse for the rest of the night. I think the most surreal moment was when I was dancing around with Daniel to 'Living on a Prayer'. We even got stopped trying to get into the dodgiest nightclub in Sydney. Daniel was such a gentleman and even invited us to his show in Adelaide the following week. We went along and he made us go backstage after the show. We were brought into his dressing room where he signed postcards for us and we took photos. He even remembered our names. Needless to say the folks back home were delighted with the photos.

*How mad is that!*
Noirin, Cork

# SINKING FEELING

While on holiday in Australia I took a trip to Frasier Island and managed to sink my jeep. I spent six hours in the water hoping to drive to freedom. I also got a tow truck and sunk that. I killed six mango trees in the process and there's a fine of $50,000 a tree for doing that.

In the end we had to get a barge in with another tow truck on top of it to pull the first tow truck out in high tide. Myself and my mate Dan (who can't swim) had to swim down to the jeep and connect the tow truck cable. Two weeks later with lighter pockets we rolled into Sydney and sold the jeep to a greasy used car salesman.

What we didn't know at the time was that the waters around Frasier Island are infested with Tiger sharks. We found that out after the tow truck drivers had thrown us out into the water to fish the jeep out.

*How mad is that!*

John

# *Caddyshock*

Myself and one of my friends were in San Sebastian in the North of Spain. There were two, let's say not the most beautiful, Americans in the campsite. I did my duty and kissed one of them. However my friend took it one step further and ended up having full relations with the other in a tent with seven other people in it during the early hours of the morning. The Americans left the next day. We thought it would be the last we saw of them.

Two years later we were both working in a bar in the west of Ireland and one of the weird old golf caddies from the local golf course brought in two young American girls with the promise of meeting some boys their own age. Who were they only the two Americans who we had met two years ago.

*How mad is that!*

# Flattery Gets You...

The Ray D'Arcy Show
WINNER

I AM A THIRD YEAR student in NUI Maynooth, doing history and economics. I write a fortnightly column for the students union newspaper, *The Spoke*. For some time I have been meaning to write an article about you, after having just discovered your brilliant radio show recently.

There was an ulterior motive to writing the article – to get a Bobblehead Ray. It is true that I thought of the article before I knew of the bobbleheads but when I heard you talking about them on air I decided to write the article after all. I know that's very presumptuous of me but I really really want a Bobblehead Ray.

I thought that by spreading the good word about you it would entice you to give me one.

Ciaran McCabe

# NEWSPAPER MADS...

# On a Wing and a Prayer

A pilot flew for over two hours before realising he had only one complete wing. He was unaware that he had hit a tree on take-off from Brittas House airstrip near Shannon, and torn nearly two metres off the left wing of his Cessna 210.

# Clean Machine

The following car advert appeared in an Irish newspaper recently:

*'Ford Puma, 1999. Red 79k alloys all elec one spotless owner. €8,000.'*

## Bagging Bargains

Ireland's €115 million lottery winner Dolores McNamara said that the purchase that has made her happiest since her massive win was a bargain bag she picked up for £25 in London – even though she could buy 4,600,000 of them.

## *Oldsmobile*

Irish mobile phone thieves have turned all nostalgic. They're turning their noses up at modern mobile phones and targeting ones you can't buy in the shops anymore.

The Nokia 330i was the biggest selling phone in Ireland until it was taken off the market. Now gardai have warned people with the old Nokia to be careful because thieves target them for the large resale price.

# SuRpRiSe!

I was on Bondi Beach at Christmas two years ago. I don't know if you have ever seen Bondi Beach on Christmas day but it is absolutely packed. You can't see the sand for towels, tents etc. My friend and I managed to find a spare patch of sand to set down our towels and begin our day of partying in the 30 degree weather. There was an empty towel to our right, but otherwise we were surrounded by people only inches away. Obviously in such close proximity to these people, we began laughing and joking quite loudly with the people around us. The next thing I know I hear someone saying my name.

'Amy?'

Now, I come from Halifax, Nova Scotia and it's not such a big place. And who is standing on the empty towel that we plonked beside but a friend of mine from university that I didn't even know was in Australia. He was there all alone with nobody to spend Christmas with and we happened to sit next to him on a beach so full of people that you couldn't find someone even with mobile phones and flares for God's sake!

*How mad is that!*
Amy Andresen

# EASTER FUNNY

I work as a gardener and usually take my holidays in January or February. In January 2004 I was lucky enough to travel to Easter Island in the Pacific Ocean. It is the most remote island in the world being 3,700km from Chile and 4,050km from Tahiti, the next nearest island.

When I was strolling around one afternoon I met two Irish girls. It was so hot we went to shelter in a local bar. Within five minutes four older people came and sat in the same area. We heard their accents and realising they were Irish too introduced ourselves to them – three Irish ladies and one Welsh man on their holidays. In the space of ten minutes I had met five Irish women on the most remote island in the world.

However the best was yet to come. As we chatted I found out that one of the ladies lives only five minutes away from me in Churchtown in Dublin. She's since become one of my gardening customers. Not only that it turned out I had once done some gardening for an uncle of one of the two girls about three years before that.

What are the chances of meeting someone who lives five minutes around the corner on the most remote island in the world?

*How mad is that!*
Colm Gallagher

# *Good Cop*

In 2001 I went to America and got a bus to Newark Train station from the airport. It was eleven at night and the station was crawling with junkies. I was nervous after such a long flight.

Then the unbelievable happened.

Two junkies came over to us and asked to carry our bags up the steps. I politely said 'no thanks' even though I was laden down.

I expected my friend to do likewise but instead he decided to hand over his bag and they carried it up the stairs. When we reached the top they asked him for money. I told him to give them some of the quarters we had just got changed to call home, but he decided otherwise.

He proceeded to lift his T-shirt and expose his hidden bumbag stuffed with $1,500 in

$100 and $50 bills. He handed over the dollar and the junkies walked away. Within 20 seconds we were surrounded by a gang who were up to no good.

One of them told us to hand over the money and just in our hour of need a local cop saw the commotion and drew his gun. The scumbags scarpered and he took us into the local station which was adjoining the train station. He gave us coffee and relaxed us and even gave us a mugshot as a souvenir.

He was a really nice guy who had Irish roots and he told us he loved Tullamore Dew whiskey. I thanked him and gave him a pack of Silk Cut as he was a smoker and it was all I could give him as a thank you!

When I returned to Ireland three months later I sent him a bottle of Tullamore Dew as I was eternally grateful. I returned to the USA two years later and one night in Queens I was playing pool with a relative when some local cops came to the table. The same cop that saved us that night was among the gang. My relative knew what had happened us when we first landed in the USA and he couldn't believe that this was the same cop who saved us.

Needless to say we drank plenty that night and even to this day I'll never forget officer Robert Noble.

*How mad is that!*
Anthony, Louth

# Sounds Familiar

I was recently in Barcelona and while there I visited the Nou Camp and did the stadium tour. During the tour we had to get a lift. I noticed the lifts were made by a company called Schindler. 'Schindlers lifts'.

*How mad is that!*
Geoff

# Ray of Sunshine

**WINNER**

I'M A 19-YEAR-OLD girl just after moving up to Dublin from Galway. So far I hate this city, everyone is rude and would walk all over you, and don't get me started on the cost of living. The highlight of my week is listening to the show for those few precious hours while slogging through work. Would you and the team take pity on a poor country girl and consider giving me a Bobblehead Ray to cheer me up when I look out the window and think of the green fields of home. It could just restore my faith in human nature.

Yours in faith
Sarah, Galway

# *Water Coincidence?*

My first name is Brita and my last name is Waters. Just like the Brita water filters.
*How mad is that!*
Brita

## RePeAt AfTer Me

My name is Kelly Magee and when I get married I will become Kelly Kelly.
*How mad is that!*
Kelly

# Handyman

I WAS PUTTING a wing on a car and the bonnet fell, trapping my hands. I had to stay there for over an hour til someone came home and let me out.

Maybe not mad but very sore!

Nearly as bad as the time I tried to take off a sweat shirt while driving ... not a good idea.

*How mad is that!*

Aidan

The Ray D'Arcy Show

WINNER

# Watch the Bend!

True story. I had a car accident a few years ago with a Yank. I'm Irish and from Donegal. His name was Randal Fastabend.

*How mad is that!*

Grace, Donegal

# *Kiely Unlikely*

My maiden name is Kiely. Then I married a Kiely and I also work for Kiely's meats in Waterford. Before I got married if I had to go to the chemist for medicine for my daughter it was typed as Kiely, Kiely. (I'm not related to any of the families.)

*How mad is that!*

# DoUbLE CeLEbRaTiON

Last February it was my birthday on a Saturday. Everyday during that week I eagerly awaited the post for cards from my family. When the post on Friday came and went without anything for me I was raging. On Friday evening a woman came to the door asking to speak to me. In her hand she held a load of envelopes. She had the same name as me and it was her birthday the following day. She lived in the road behind me with the same number as mine.

*How mad is that!*
Fiona O'Sullivan

# NEWSPAPER MADS...

## Sounds Wealthy!

The National Lottery announced that a young man from Kildare won €450,000 in the weekend lotto draw. The newly wealthy lad bought the lucky ticket in the Mace store in Prosperous!

## Dickheads!

An English bank has apologised to a teenager after sending him a bankcard with the words Dick Head embossed on it.

Chris Lancaster, 18, only spotted the error when he whipped out his card at the local Tesco.

# NEWSPAPER MADS...

## *Stained Window*

Experts who examined a stained glass window in a Killarney church have discovered Ireland's oldest graffiti.

The manger scene window in St. Mary's Church was thought to include a bearded Christ child.

But stained glass expert David Lawrence identified the 100-year-old doodle as graffiti and removed it with white spirits and cotton wool.

## Offaly Hot!

A place that sounds like it's freezing is proving to be Ireland's hot spot.

The last thing you would say is 'Brrrr!' in Birr County Offaly. It is the warmest place to be in Ireland according to the Met Office.

# NEWSPAPER MADS...

## No Joy!

A SURVEY has revealed that women called Joy are the most likely to make insurance claims. The next two most likely names are Diana and Tracey. The unluckiest man's name is Sean. The unluckiest names were compiled when English insurance company Churchill surveyed 200,000 claims.

# Nappy Landings

When I was 18 months old I fell 10 feet and had a bike fall on top of me. I obviously survived but – here's the mad thing – all that was marked were my hands with scratches and some bruises. They think my nappy broke my fall.

*How mad is that!*
Ciara, Cork

# Waste Disposal

When I was five I wanted a 'doll that pees' for Christmas but to my horror I got a Timmy Doll. I kicked up such a fuss Timmy's peeing mechanism had to be cut off.

*How mad is that!*

# Dirty Secret

BACK IN THE DAYS when you were presenting *The Den*, I appeared on the birthday photographs. Now this is nothing weird in itself, except my mam decided to send in a picture of me doing the hoovering in the house. As you can imagine this was highly embarrassing for an

eight-year-old boy. But the psychological scars wore off and I got on with my life.

Then about three years ago I was walking down Griffith Avenue in Dublin when who did I see but yourself driving the opposite way. What freaked me out totally was the fact that I was carrying a hoover from my own house to my friends.

So basically the two times I could be associated with you, I've been holding a hoover of all things.

*How mad is that!*
Eoin McNamara

# Master Pilot

When I was nine or ten on a flight home from London with Aer Lingus I was let into the cockpit. I was allowed to stay there for the landing and actually pressed a button during the landing. What a day. Only a kid and helping to land a huge plane.

*How mad is that!*

# Tears at Seven

When I was seven years old there was an advert on the TV for life assurance. The music that was on it was Louis Armstrong's 'We've got all the time in the world.'

Everytime it would come on I'd see the advert and hear the music and start crying.

*How mad is that!*
Shane, Clare

# WOULD YOU BELIEVE

When I was five I thought an acorn at the bottom of the stream in Glendalough was a baby crocodile. I was laughed at by about 50 Chinese tourists.

*How mad is that!*
Niall, Laois

# Cliffhanger

When I was eight the family went on a day out to the Cliffs of Moher. While walking along I lost my footing and ended up hanging from the side of the cliff for dear life. My sister just stood there laughing at me, while my mother came close to her death trying to pull me back up, so my dad had to pull the two of us back over to safety. I will never forget that.

*How mad is that!*
David, Galway

# CHEST PAINS

When I was five I thought there was buried treasure in the house next door because the people who owned the house were from America and there was a trunk in one of the bedrooms. But I thought I was a pirate etc. so I convinced my cousin that we should break in. We proceeded to the shed, while my parents were in the house and took a hammer and a chair and carried it out next door. I broke the window, the glass shattered and I cut my thigh. It was really deep and I should have got stitches, but instead I hid it for days. Needless to say they found the burglar. I never got the stitches and I still have a really big scar on my thigh.

*How mad is that!*
Claire from Clare

# Terrible Twos

When I was two I was in hospital for an operation and was sleeping in a cot with bars. I escaped one night and made it to the front door only to be caught by the dinner lady. I can still see the traffic outside the hospital door.

*How mad is that!*

# HeAdAcHE

When my sister was young she had problems going to the loo, doing her number twos. The only way she could go was if my mum squeezed her head. So basically she would sit there being squeezed by the head 'til she was done. She is 18 now, though I'm sure she squeezes her own head now.

*How mad is that!*
Tommy, Wexford

# LITTLE SQUIRT

We grew up living over my father's grocery shop. Back in the 60s and 70s the modern and efficient housewife could purchase her Colman's English Mustard in a tube, just like the toothpaste tube. My brother's favourite pastime was to grab a handful of tubes of mustard and go sit in the garden squirting the mustard into his mouth and eating it. My eyes water just thinking of it.

*How mad is that!*

Gordon, Westmeath

# The Name's Lennon, James Lennon

I was an extra in a movie called *Zardos*, starring Sean Connery, filmed in Ardmore Studios and around Wicklow in 1972. I was three years old and I filmed a very brief scene with 'Uncle Sean' and was in the film for approximately five seconds.

I was an extra again in another movie, *The First Great Train Robbery*, in which he starred with Donald Sutherland, in about 1982. When Sean Connery finished filming a scene he was heading back to the dressing room when our tapdancing teacher, Nuala Moiselle, spotted him and dragged us over. She called him and he stopped for a chat. During the conversation I asked him if he remembered me from *Zardos* and he said 'James, of course I remember him. He sure has grown.'

Sean Connery remembered me.

*How mad is that!*

James Lennon, Dublin

# TOP SOIL

I was having lunch in Kilkenny Design Centre in Kilkenny with my friend and our two daughters who were about three at the time. We had just finished lunch and our daughters went to the stairwell in the restaurant. A minute or so later my daughter said that she had gone to the toilet – and that she did it over there. I asked her was it a piddle – and she said no. I went over to pick it up quickly with a tissue and hopefully not too many people would notice. As I tried to pick it up I noticed she had a touch of diarrhoea and had to ask for water and disinfectant, as the American tourists tried not to notice the smell.

*How mad is that!*

Andrea

# Fog Warning

ABOUT 40 YEARS AGO when I was a nipper my parents got fed up calling or looking for me around the estate when it was dinner, tea or bedtime. So my father, God rest his soul, hit on an idea. He had an old World War II foghorn which he mounted on the coal shed wall and when it was time for me to come home he would give it a couple of blasts. You could hear the bloody yoke for miles around.

*How mad is that!*
Dave

# Plan Backfires

When I was 11 my granny passed away and after the funeral my granddad had people back to the house. He used one of the fields as a car park for the day and the local inn provided the food. They had chocolate éclairs for dessert and the caterers would only allow me and my cousin to have one helping. We knew the house like the back of our hand, and we were able to sneak into the room where they were keeping the food and managed to rob a whole tray of éclairs.

My cousin and I dashed to the field where all the cars were and proceeded to stuff our faces. But our eyes were bigger than our bellies and we had a problem. We were only a quarter way through the éclairs and we knew we couldn't finish them all or bring back the tray with the remaining éclairs.

We then had a great idea to stuff them up the exhaust pipes of the parked cars. Satisfied with the empty tray we went back to the house. After a while we thought our great idea wasn't so great for the cars so we decided to ask our uncle, 'What could happen to a car if someone put a chocolate éclair in the exhaust pipe?' He goes 'You little bastards get out and get those éclairs out of the cars.'

When we went back out a lot of the cars had left. The field was a mess with soot-covered cream and dough, and cars parked behind the cars with éclairs had cream splattered on them. It was a mess. We were in trouble and we did our best cleaning the mess. But at least the cows had an interesting meal.

*How mad is that!*

Conor Malone

# FIRST LOVE

I was staying in the Barrettstown Camp twelve years ago and Ray was down as a guest.

He was sitting at our table and we were having a great laugh with him. I was around twelve at the time. I told Ray I fancied a girl I met there earlier that week.

Later that night Ray was talking on stage giving out awards, when out of the blue I heard him mention about chatting to me at the table and how I talked all about Emma – the girl I fancied.

In front of 150 people all the same age he called her and me up and got her to give me a kiss! Only for the facepaint I would have been glowing like the sun.

I still have scars to this day and can never speak about a girl to a lad in confidence again.

*How mad is that!*

Emotionally scarred young man

# Cardinal Error

WHEN I WAS FOUR I was at a ceremony where my mam's friend was being made a bishop. Cardinal Cathal Daly was there.

I was four and I had a naked Barbie doll with me. I showed the Cardinal my Barbie's boobies.

*How mad is that!*
Deirdre, Limerick

The Ray D'Arcy Show
**WINNER**

# Born on the 4th of July

GET THIS. Tis American Independence Day and not only is it my birthday, but I have a twin sister and it's her birthday too. Born a twin on Independence Day!

*How mad is that!*

Celine Barber, Dublin

# InPeCtOr FrOsTiE

One day, when we were 12, my friend and I cycled to the shop to spend our pocket money on sweets. We didn't have much money so all we could afford was a packet of Frosties each. On the way home I was devastated to discover that I had dropped my Frosties along the road somewhere. After about half an hour of frantic searching my friend and I gave up. I was gutted.

My friend had a bright idea. She would walk to where I discovered my Frosties were missing, turn around, throw her own packet of Frosties randomly behind her and see where they landed. Strange I know, as she risked losing her own packet of cereal too. However we decided to give it a shot. I watched my friend's Frosties land in the hedge, I raced to the spot and lo and behold the two packets of Frosties were lying only inches apart.

*How mad is that!*

Donna, Monaghan

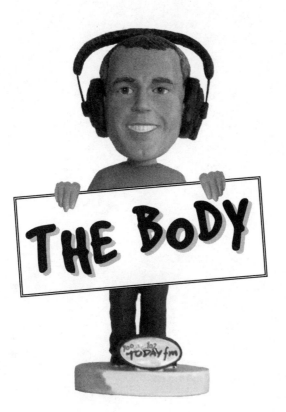

# *Carrot Topped*

I was mashing carrots for my baby when a carrot flew out of the pot, stuck to my head and now I have a huge blister on my forehead.

*How mad is that!*

Kitty

# SQUIDICULOUS

I have an irrational fear of squids and octopuses because they look like sea scrotums.

*How mad is that!*

Al

# PLENTY OF GARGLE

In 1986 I was taken into St. James hospital late at night with a bleeding ulcer. After completing all the examinations they brought me to a ward so the specialist could see me in the morning. I asked for a drink of water, as the thirst was becoming unbearable. The nurses couldn't risk giving me a drink, as I may have needed an operation the next morning so they kept putting my request on the long finger.

So at three in the morning I'm facing this snoring guy across the ward who has on his bedside locker all the bottles of minerals left in the world, while the only things in my locker are two empty plastic cups (meant for false teeth). As far as I was concerned the only person who could have put those cups there was God.

I unhooked the saline drip from the stand and bummed my way across the ward as quickly as possible, said sorry to my loudly snoring pal and poured a plastic cupful of 7UP. Back in bed, hooked up again I began the slowest and most enjoyable gargle of my life. Using the two cups, I took a mouthful of 7UP, gargled so as to get the full sensation on my tastebuds and then spat it out into the other cup. When I had it all transferred into the second cup I put it back in the locker and lay down to go asleep.

*How mad is that!*

Christy Nolan

# NEWSPAPER MADS...

## *Speedy Burial*

Mourners at a recent funeral didn't get much rest and repose.

Stunned family members looked on in horror as the remains of their beloved was careered around the graveyard by stampeding funeral horses. They have settled a damages claim against the undertaker.

The wheel came off the hearse and the coffin was also severely damaged during the rampage by the horses.

# Don't Kiss and Make-Up

Applying endless amounts of make-up could be a waste of time – if you do it to attract men.

A survey has found that men find women with heavy make-up a real turn off.

Over two thirds of men, a staggering 65%, are put off by females who wear heavy make-up. And 34% of men are irritated by women's lengthy cosmetic rituals while away.

# Turf's Up!

I was told that I was going to the bog to turn turf. Before I went that morning I gave myself my usual haircut, a grade zero. I spent three hours turning turf during the hottest day of the year so far. I went home and my head started heating up and getting sorer.

I asked my wife did she have any cooling creams I could put on my head. She pulled out a spray and said it was perfect and started spraying my head. It cooled my head down straight away.

A few hours later my head was stinging again so I went up to the bedroom and started spraying this cooling cream on my head again. Not only did I spray it on but also I started rubbing it in with my hands, making sure all my head was cooled down.

When I woke up on Sunday morning there was a smell in the bed of tanning cream. My hands were deep brown in patches. I jumped out of bed and looked in the mirror and my head was tanned. I had put tanning cream on! I scrubbed my head and hands but my wife pointed out that fake tan doesn't scrub out.

I had to go to work on Monday and the first mate I met reckoned it looked like someone had crapped on my head and rubbed it in.

On Tuesday my head started to flake a little, and another mate said you could see a tide mark along one side of my head.

It's Wednesday today and I'm writing to you with three distinct colours on the top of my head: brown where the tan is left, beetroot red where my head was not tanned and finally white where the scalp has flaked.

*How mad is that!*
Joe

117

# EyE DoN't BeLiEvE It!

A carpenter living by me has a glass eye. He was putting up rafters with a workmate. To check if it was level the trade said 'Put your eye on that.' Packie took his eye out and put it on the rafter. It frightened the shite out of your man as they had only just met.

*How mad is that!*

Danny

**The Ray D'Arcy Show**

**WINNER**

# Rear Ended

ABOUT THREE YEARS AGO when I was getting a lift off a mate of mine in the back of his van he decided to drive over a speed bump a little faster than he should have and I flew straight up into the air and then thumped back down on my arse. After about two days of agony I decided to go to the doctor to discover that I had broken about three quarters of an inch of my coccyx. I spent the next three weeks in agony, not being able to sit down.

*How mad is that!*

Shane, Kerry

## Drink, Feck...

A bishop stunned kids when he claimed: 'There's no point taking the pledge – half of you probably drink already.' The bishop advised youngsters in Kilkenny – who were about to take the pledge – not to make any decision on alcohol until they were at least 16 years old.

## When I am Old...

A study by NUI Galway has revealed that people as old as 92 are still having regular sex. The study quizzed 69 people and the majority of participants in the study who were over 70 said sex was still a very important part of their lives.

**NEWSPAPER MADS...**

# Not Tonight, Dear

Snorers have never been popular but the results of a recent survey could mean they will lose even more sleep.

People who snore have sexual intercourse less often than others according to a survey. More than a quarter hardly ever have sex and 60% are regularly told to sleep in the spare room.

# Undercover

My good friend and work colleague here in Heatmerchants in Athlone went out celebrating her birthday on Easter bank holiday Monday and due to some severe over indulgence, had a sudden and dire urge to urinate in the bushes of Kilmartins N6 service station. However, after due consideration the following morning we came to the conclusion that there are no bushes at Kilmartins N6 service station . . .

*How mad is that!!*
Thanks and regards
Sandra Lynch

# Pissed as a Newt

WHEN I WAS FIRST with my boyfriend of

three years he revealed
to me that he thought
women peed out of
their vaginas. I went on
to explain the facts to
him and referring to the
newly discovered hole I
said 'No one would
blame you for not
knowing. It's minute.'

One day we were
talking about roughly the
same subject when he
referred to my anatomy
innocently as 'your newt'. I was confused and
when he used it again I quizzed him further. He
got a bit annoyed and said 'You called it your
newt not me!'

*How mad is that!*
Ann Marie

# NEWSPAPER MADS...

## *Locked!*

A New Hampshire man tried for two weeks to remove a padlock from his testicles with a hacksaw. He had fallen asleep during a drinking session and woke up with the delicately positioned padlock.

After a fortnight he gave up and went to his local hospital.

## Fallen Comrades

At a State ceremony in the Royal Hospital Kilmainham to remember fallen army comrades four cadets in the guard of honour fainted in the sweltering heat.

**NEWSPAPER MADS...**

# Does my Dummy Look Big in This?

It's not just fashions that constantly change – Irish shop dummies have to keep up with the times too.

Makers of fashion mannequins have been forced to make dummies with bigger bottoms and chests to keep pace with changing attitudes to female beauty. American dummy designers have even consulted curvy Jennifer Lopez about the changes.

# NEWSPAPER MADS...

# Do You Take This CD...?

Catholic Church officials have launched their own album of suitable wedding tracks in an attempt to stop inappropriate music at weddings.

*Waterloo*, *I Don't Know How to Love Him* and *Will You Still Love Me Tomorrow* have been some of the more unsuitable tracks used by couples at their weddings.

The church CD of suitable songs includes *On Eagles Wings* and *Morning Has Broken*.

## NEWSPAPER MADS...

# *Is That a Truncheon in your Pocket?*

Police officers are to mingle with bathers on a nudist beach in a bid to catch perverts.

The officers will wear swimming costumes at Studland Beach, Dorset in a bid to prevent naturists from being approached for exhibitionist sex, known as 'dogging.'

# Deadly Music

Ireland's state pathologist Marie Cassidy has revealed that she listens to country crooner Daniel O'Donnell while dissecting bodies.

When she tires of wee Daniel she pops on a Tom Jones CD. 'You can be working on a body for eight hours and you have to have humour to keep everyone's spirits up.'

# Picture That

I met a guy on holidays a few years back. Although he lived on the other side of the city we went on a few dates when we got back home. We were together a few weeks and he decided it was time to introduce me to his friends. One weekend a friend of his had a house party in his parent's house when they were away. I was sitting in the living room having the craic when I looked on the windowsill and saw a holiday snap of a gang of people. Looking at it closer I couldn't believe it – I was in the picture! Next thing I knew, the party host's sister came into the living room – she was a girl I had met on holidays in Eastern Europe when I was 15. Before I knew, we had her old holiday album out and were reminiscing about the holiday.

*How mad is that!*

Rachel

# YoU tOo?

On the Friday before the U2 concert in Croke park I was speaking to my next-door neighbour in the garden. He said he was going to U2 on Monday. I told him that Laura and myself were going the same night. He said he was in the Canal End stand with his girlfriend. So were we. I said get your tickets and we will see if we are near each other. The seats were right beside each other: S320, Row AA 12, 13, 14 and 15.

*How mad is that!*
Frank McMahon

# ANY PORT IN A STORM

Fate is the only reason that I am on this planet. Years ago my father worked as a radio officer on ships. He travelled around the world but one day he got word that his brother was emigrating to New Zealand. Back then when you left for faraway lands you were usually gone for good so my dad asked for leave to go home and say goodbye to his brother. They refused him but he fought hard and eventually they let him off the ship on Friday for a week's holiday. Saturday night the ship broke its back in a storm and sank – all the crew members were lost, including the poor guy who had just got on the ship to replace Dad.

If Dad's brother hadn't been emigrating that week – I wouldn't be here!

*How mad is that!*
Michelle Gildea

# Old Flame

I was in my local pub a few years ago having a drink with some locals and my father. There was a stranger sitting on the far side of my father and as they were talking the subject turned to work and father said that he supplied fire extinguishers. The stranger said that he was born about eight miles away and always remembers a knock on the door of the house late one night when he was small and a man was there saying that there were huge flames coming from the chimney. He had in his hands a couple of fire extinguishers and he came in and put the fire out. Shortly afterwards the fire brigade arrived (neighbours had seen the flames and called them). But when they got there the fire was out and there was no sign of the man with the extinguishers.

It turned out my father was driving home from work one night and had seen the chimney on fire and stopped because he had extinguishers in the car. The fire brigade arrived and he didn't want to be in the way so he left. The people that owned the house never knew who he was. Then 20 or more years later one of the family, who was only eleven at the time, and my father met as complete strangers in the local pub.

*How mad is that!*
Aidan Browne

# Snookered

Alex Higgins walked into a bar I was working in a few years ago. He was there to meet his friend Oliver Reid. Alex heard the breaking of balls at a pool table and asked if he could play. I took him through and he gave an exhibition of pool, and then he took people on for £1 a game. After a couple of those I took him on and beat him. I took the pound coin from him. Just then Oliver walked in and took him away. Alex shook my hand and said he'd be back for his rematch. He never came back. I took the coin to a local steel factory where I had a hole put in it and it's on my key set since.

*How mad is that?*

Pat Barrett, Limerick

# NEWSPAPER MADS...

# Eye'll See You in Court

A publican who took out his false eye and threw it at a Garda recently received a prison sentence.

The man in question had been drinking heavily when he walked into his local Garda station, put his eye on a counter and slammed his fist to make it bounce up and down.

# NoT sEpArAtEd At BiRtH

My first story begins on the 11th of May 1970 when Mary Lucey from Knocknagree in County Cork makes her way to the Bons Secour Hospital in Cork City to have her first child. Imagine her surprise when in the ward alongside her is another Mary Lucey from Birr in County Offaly who was giving birth to a child of her own. Both ladies gave birth to two bouncing baby girls and there were lots of jokes on the ward about not mixing up the two babies.

Fast-forward 26 years later to the Eye, Ear, Nose and Throat hospital on Adelaide Road in Dublin. Sheila Courtney (nee Lucey) now aged 25, a staff nurse at the hospital, gets selected along with five other nurses to study for a diploma in ophthalmic nursing. One of the other girls on the course is Sonia Lucey. Sheila mentions to Sonia after a few days that her maiden name is Lucey. They then started talking about birthdays. Imagine their surprise when they discover that they share the same birthday – the 11th May. Yes, Ray, after almost 26 years Baby Lucey 1 and Baby Lucey 2 are reunited.

What are the odds that both these girls would have chosen nursing as a career, would go to work in Dublin, and that they would have been one of only six nurses chosen to study the same course?

*How mad is that!*

Mike Courtney

# TALES OF THE UNEXPECTED

When I was 10 or so I had *The Giraffe, The Pelly and Me*, a great book by Roald Dahl. I loved this book and read it about 10,000 times. On the inside cover I wrote my name and all the names of the members of my family.

One day, when my mother was cleaning out the house, she gave away the book along with a load of other stuff to a charity shop. I was devastated and even a shiny new copy bought by my dad didn't put me in better humour.

Fourteen years later, while at a car boot sale, my mother saw a copy of *The Giraffe, the Pelly and Me* on sale. When she opened the cover there was my name and all the rest of the family's names.

*How mad is that!*
Donal O'Brien

140

# *Sacre Blue!*

I recently found out that my brother's French wife (they have been married for five years) came to Ireland 25 years ago for a French exchange with an Irish family.

My fiancée and I were looking through photos of this trip with his wife when my fiancée recognised the table in the background. It was her family my sister-in-law exchanged with. Lo and behold my fiancée saw herself in nappies several pictures on!

*How mad is that!*

Rory McKeown

# NEWSPAPER MADS....

## *Sign of the Times*

An unwitting health worker in the Department of Health was paid €1 million by mistake. The computer system in the Department did not pick up the error and it only came to light when the employee noticed the extra money in their account and told their employer.

Minister for Health Mary Harney admitted there were 'serious concerns' about the department's computer system.

# Table Service

My girlfriend and I were sitting in a bar in Boston having a bite to eat when Shane McGowan approached us wanting the pickles from our plates. He serenaded my girlfriend and then took the pickles. So Shane McGowan actually sang for his supper.

*How mad is that!*

Garrett, Cork

# GlEeSoN's GLOry

I was in work and my mate and I were trying to remember Brendan Gleeson's character in *Troy*. The man himself came into the shop and settled it for us. It's a true story and we saved the CCTV footage.

*How mad is that!*

143

# Lost and Found

ABOUT SIX YEARS ago, in January 1999, just after I moved to Waterford, I was walking to work one Saturday morning when I spotted a gold bracelet on the ground. I picked it up and brought it to a jewellers to have the clasp repaired. She told me that it was a very  expensive bracelet, but that the clasp was not the original clasp for the bracelet. I kept the bracelet and wore it for a few years.

Fast forward to January 2005. I was having a drink one night with a couple that we had met after moving to Waterford. Myself and Olivia got talking about the first presents our partners had given us. I told her the first present I received from Ciaran, my husband, was a gold bracelet, and I showed her. She then told me that she had also received a gold bracelet from her partner for their first Christmas together. Unfortunately she had lost it years ago. She then went on to describe it to me and showed me the matching necklace that she had gotten for it. It suddenly dawned on me that the bracelet I had found six years ago was actually hers. She was so shocked she wouldn't believe it until I showed it to her.

*How mad is that!*

Fiona Jordan

# NEWSPAPER MADS...

## Top Hat

Two holy hats of a deceased priest have been ascribed healing powers. The hats of the late Fr. John McWey are held by two Offaly residents.

Many people sit alone with the hat in a room and say a prayer or ask for Fr. McWey to intercede on their behalf.

# NEWSPAPER MADS...

## *Rainy Day Fund*

It is estimated that Irish people have hoarded €40 million worth of euro coins in jars, piggy banks, dresser drawers and sofas.

According to a recent survey 60% of Irish households keep a coin jar or container and amass about €300 per year in stored change.

## Slim Chance of Success

Curvy women are more successful at work than their skinny counterparts, according to a new survey.

Bosses who were surveyed said that curvy women are 'more appealing, seem healthier and are more relaxed and at ease with themselves'.

# Corr Blimey!

Four years ago my wife, Edel, and I went on a holiday to Australia. We covered the usual tracks, but it was our trip to Ayres Rock that was pretty weird.

We flew there from Melbourne and landed on the smallest piece of tarmac I've ever seen.

We got a minibus to Ayres Rock the next morning and were joined by a guy with a London accent, who said his name was Tom.

He asked me if I was Irish and said his dad was from Ireland.

'He went to London about 40 years ago and met my mum over there. So where are you guys from?' he asked.

'Cavan. It's about 100km from Dublin. You probably never heard of it,' I said.

It turned out that that's where his dad was from. Not only that, his father was from Ballinagh, where I'm from!

'So what's his name?' I said.

'Thomas Corr,' he replied.

'My granny's name was Corr,' I said.

We traced it all back and realised that Tom and I were actually second cousins. He was on a career break and was travelling around the world.

What are the chances of us ending up in a minibus together on the other side of the world at 4.30am on a Tuesday?

*How mad is that!*

Neil Keogan, Dublin

# IT's A miraClE

I got on a plane in Knock with my sister and she took out the book she was reading, *Pride and Prejudice*. She opened it somewhere in the middle. A woman then sat down beside us and took out the same book and we looked at each other in amazement when she opened it on the exact same page.

*How mad is that!*
Michael O'Donnell

# *Silver Lining*

I worked in London with MRS refuse collectors. One day myself and the driver went into a pub during work hours. We did not take any notice of the camera crew that were nearby. A few weeks later we were called into the bosses office to be told we were on a week's suspension as we were drinking during work hours. We denied this until we were shown the previous evening's episode of *The Bill* and the driver and myself were in the background going into the pub!

As one must, I had to drown my sorrows in the local in Kilburn. A new barmaid had started that day and as you do, I gave all the best lines to impress just in case I might get lucky. To my surprise they worked and we are now married and expecting our seventh baby.

*How mad is that!*

# GrEaT MinDs

My best friend Lisa and I have been living together for years now. Over those years there were times when we said the same things, went to pick up the same things or do the same things at the same time. It was always a laugh at the time as we thought we had some telepathic thing going on.

There was this one time that stands out very much from the other times. We went to Domino's to get a pizza one night. As I waited for the pizza Lisa went to the shop next door to pick up some things. When I came out of Domino's I went to get into a different car. As I was the driver I tried putting the key in to open the driver's door. When I copped on I was quite embarrassed so quickly ran to my own car and got in laughing to myself.

About two minutes later Lisa came to my car laughing. 'You will never guess what I did,' she said. She went over to the same car and tried to get into it. She also legged it when she realised.
*How mad is that!*
Emma

**NEWSPAPER MADS...**

# Soft Touch

A leading insurance broker has said that insurance premiums are dropping in Dublin because thieves are now decentralising.

According to Michael Downes an underwriter with FBD, 'Burglars are stealing cars in Dublin and driving them down the country to do the houses there. They find them easier to get in and out of,' adding that most Dublin houses are now fitted with deadbolts.

# NEWSPAPER MADS...

## Young Turks

Three women have been awarded €500 each because they were refused entry to a pub for being too old.

Two sisters and their friend tried to get into trendy Dublin pub the Turk's Head but were refused. The Equality Tribunal ordered the payout.

## Sunbathers Anonymous

There may be another reason why we just can't stop sunbathing – we may be addicted to it.

Using criteria adapted from an alcoholism screening questionnaire, researchers concluded that 26% of those surveyed could be classed as 'ultraviolet light tanning dependent.'

# SPIDER SENSE

I met my boyfriend nine years ago. Paul was in college in Dublin but he dropped out just after we met and went back to Louth. A few days after leaving Dublin he phoned me. I had been zoning out staring at this Daddy Long Legs on the windowsill and thinking how weird they look. As soon as I picked up the phone Paul asked me had I ever noticed how strange Daddy Long Legs are. He was sitting staring at one too.

*How mad is that!*
Sheena

# No Man is a (Greek) Island

A few years ago my brother was holidaying in Greece. One day he got drunk and fell asleep in the sun, and cooked like a goose at Christmas. A woman who was close by noticed and warned him he'd better get inside.

They began chatting and realised they were both Irish. She said she was from Mayo and asked my brother where he was from. He replied Castlebar. She asked him where in Castlebar and he said a village called Belcarra.

The woman said nothing but then said whereabouts in Belcarra and he said Lisaniskea. She seemed surprised and asked who he was. Then she said she went to school with his mother.

*How mad is that!*
Michael O'Donnell

# No(r) Way!

When I finished my Leaving Cert I got a job as an au pair with a family in Norway. I was introduced to a cousin of the family who also employed Irish au pairs. Myself and Lisa, the other Irish au pair, got talking about where we were from and our family and stuff. She mentioned she worked as a nurse in Dublin for the last few years.

We talked over tea about Ireland and a few names kept popping up. Lisa comes from south Kilkenny and I'm from south Tipperary. One name in particular Eoin came up in conversation. It was his nickname 'Stoney' that started us laughing for about an hour. She had gone out with him the same year I had and we had never met before until we both applied for the au pair jobs in Norway.

*How mad is that!*

Claire

# THE FRENCH ROSE

I was on holidays with my parents in the south of France a few weeks ago. We were at the beach and using the sun loungers when a French lady came over to take the money for the use of them.

She asked us if we were Irish. We said we were. She said her grandmother was Irish and it turned out that her granny was from the same town as us, Tralee in County Kerry.

Then we asked her what her grandmother's name was. She replied that it was Catherine Daly. That's my mother's name!

*How mad is that!*

Ailis

# CLOSE SHAVE

My friend Derek and I were out in Howth having a few drinks some years ago. He showed up that night with a new haircut. Whenever he got his hair cut it knocked years off him. You would nearly ask him if his mother knew he was out if he approached you.

After the pub we went to a nightclub. I was waved in but Derek was stopped. They said he was too young, and he couldn't produce any ID. The funny thing is we were regulars but he looks so young when he gets his hair chopped.

We ended up going to another nightclub instead and started mingling. After about 30 minutes in the club I spied a beautiful girl who I was besotted with at first sight. I told Derek how I felt and five minutes later I was dancing with her! It turned out she was his cousin.

Nine years later we are married and Derek was our best man at the wedding.

If Derek never got his hair cut that day and he never got refused from that club our paths would never have crossed.

*How mad is that!*
Neil Doherty

# This Way Up!

I was in a pub a few years ago having a pint and a chat with some mates. I decided to have a cigarette and put one in my mouth and lit it. But as I took it from my mouth I dropped it on the floor.

To my amazement there was the cigarette standing butt end on the floor. I mean it landed in a vertical position with the lighting end upwards.

*How mad is that!*
Ray McInerney, Clare

# Red Alert

My brother's friend's girlfriend was in Australia a few years ago and she was in the bar having a drink with her buddies. During the course of the night, she saw a girl at the bar in a red cardigan that she really admired. After a while, she decided to go up to the other girl and tell her how striking the cardigan was. So she did, and that was the end of that.

Five years later, she was in Germany and was looking for an apartment and answered a random advert in the paper. She asked to view the apartment. Who answered the door only a complete stranger! BUT, when she went in to see the sitting room, what was lying on the couch only the red cardigan. And didn't yer wan from the bar only turn out to be living there. How mad is that I hear you ask. Well on a scale from 1 to MAD I'd say 'tis Fairly Mad.

Peter

# Popular Day!

THE DAY that Will left on leave, i.e. last Friday May 7th, is the same date Martin left last year. I know this because I composed a farewell poem for Martin on his last day with the line 'and so on this day the seventh of May'.

*How mad is that!*
Emma, Clare

# *Close Call*

A few years ago me and my boyfriend had an evening of passion. When he dropped me home I sent him a text making references to what happened earlier etc. Only I didn't send it to my boyfriend, I sent it to my DAD! As soon as I was sending it I realised what I had done. Then I heard his phone beeping in his bedroom. Thank God he was asleep and I was able to run in and snatch his phone and delete the message, otherwise I think I would have had a lot of awkward explaining to do.

*How mad is that!*
Loyal listener, Clare

# BaBy BrAnDy

My name is Iosaf Bennis. I have a twin brother called Eoin. When we were born in May 1978 I was born second – and quite unexpectedly for my parents! And Eoin being the stronger baby had given me a fair beating in the womb. So I was born unable to breathe! There were emergency measures taken to try and revive me.

As this was over 25 years ago the methods of reviving me were quite different from today – a nurse by the fire with me on her lap!

There was another man in the nursing home whose wife was having a child and he was settling his nerves with some brandy when he heard about my breathing troubles, so he came into the room with a teaspoon of brandy. I took my first breath with the aid of some brandy. Well 21 years later, my twin brother and I were at a 21st birthday party of his friend Claire – and lo and behold it turned out that her father was the father who had brought me my first brandy! So I made sure to meet him and buy back the round! We had a brandy each and toasted to the madness of it all!

*How mad is that!*

Iosaf Bennis, Dublin

# Double Celebration

My brother was having his daughter christened last week. We were all sitting at the top of the church waiting for it to begin when the priest announced that my brother and his girlfriend were going to get married first. Everybody was shocked – and nobody knew it was happening! We ended up having a great day, it was also my brother's birthday – a triple celebration.

*How mad is that!*

Lynn, Cork

# SMALL WORLD

I'm from New Zealand and I met my Irish wife here and we've been married now for eight years.

Two years ago we were having a drink in our local at Christmas, as you do. The next thing in walks my cousin. A bit of a shock – as she's an Aussie – and she then introduced me to her fiancé whom she met in Oz.

My wife turns around and says 'Hi Fergal, long time no see.' He was from the same town as her!

*How mad is that!*
Cheers, Shaun

# *Potty Mouth*

Ray, I bought a new bottle of mouth wash on Monday and yesterday it was half gone. I found out my granny was using it as toilet duck.

*How mad is that!*
Sharon, Carlow

# Ejector Seat

My neighbour took out the passenger seat of his car so he wouldn't have to give his brother a lift to work.

*How mad is that!*
D Finn

# Oh BrOtHeR!

Myself and the girlfriend went travelling to Oz last year for the year. At one point we were living in an apartment in Melbourne. I checked the mailbox one day there and among other letters addressed to previous tenants was a letter addressed to my girlfriend's brother. He had been in Australia two years earlier. On opening the letter we found it was a bank statement and a new bankcard. Unknown to us he had lived in the same apartment and the bank was reissuing a new card.

*How mad is that!*

Garrett Stewart

PS: He had only five dollars in the account.

# WHAT A SEND OFF

I told my girlfriend that I had to go away for work for a week so I could jet off with the lads to the States – and I bumped into her parents in the airport.

*How mad is that!*

# Tummy Bulb

After a night out on the booze my younger sister brought a load of friends home for a few drinks. She made steak sandwiches for everyone – frying steaks, chopping onions, ketchup the works! After about half an hour one of her mates started to get sick.

She questioned my mother about it the next day to find if the steaks were gone off. She said they were bought fresh that day. After a little investigation my mother eventually found out that the onions my sister chopped up and fried in butter were actually her daffodil bulbs.

*How mad is that!*

Barry Hicka

# *Eye Strain*

I have a phobia about getting a paper cut on my eyeball. It got so bad in college that I had to walk in the middle of the corridors because I was afraid that a poster hanging on the wall would, due to the force of air moving when I passed, flap up and cut my eyeball. I got a paper cut recently on my finger and I had to take a day off work I was so traumatised. I have managed to control my fear but I take it day by day!

*How mad is that!*

Justin, Galway

PS: If you send me a Bobblehead please don't send me a cover letter, as in my excitement I might accidentally rip open the envelope and the letter might fly out and cut my eyeball!

# Code-Ology

OVER THE NEXT FEW YEARS the government will spend millions of euro to add postcodes to Irish addresses to allow for easier delivering. As you may have already noticed, the address on the envelope you are holding is missing three very important pieces of information; the street address, the city address and the county address, yet you have received my letter. What good is an extra address line going to do if you can still receive my letter with practically no address?

*How mad is that!*

Ian

# FaMiLy ReUnIoN

After a company night out in Shannon, I met up with a few people I knew vaguely that I had met in the local nightclub. I missed the company bus back to Limerick where I live, so I followed them to a house where the family were on holiday, except for one of the children, who was holding a party.

I thought it was weird we had to get in through the window – but was reassured that the guy of the house was coming soon.

While sitting on the couch and settling into my first few beers I started to have a look around and was shocked to see photos of my uncle and family all over the walls. It was my uncle's house and there were still people coming in the windows at that stage.

*How mad is that!*
Keith

# NEWSPAPER MADS...

## Help Wanted

Celtic Tiger workers, too busy to do the most basic of housekeeping tasks, are paying others to do them instead. A new Dublin company is offering to organise your dry cleaning, drop back rented DVDs and even bring cars for NCTs and repairs.

## Poor Po-ouch!

A dog has made a full recovery after 350 bladderstones were removed during emergency surgery.

The Shih Tzu named Carrie was thought to be suffering from a bladder infection. Some of the stones were as big as golf balls while others were the size of a grain of sand.

# QUEUE LOOK FAMILIAR

I lost my grandmother a few years ago. We were particularly close. She had a great sense of humour and we would often joke about who we would come back to spook in the afterlife.

Recently I was at the checkout in a supermarket. There was an elderly woman in front of me and I noticed her hands looked familiar. They reminded me of my granny's hands because she had freckles on her thumb. I got a weird feeling there was a connection with her and Gran.

I followed her out and interrupted her and told her what happened. The woman turned out to be my gran's sister. She lived a good distance away from us and that's why I didn't know her.

Maybe that was my gran's way of spooking me out, but she did it in a nice way.

*How mad is that!*

# *Watching Over You*

My mother passed away earlier this year. I had been looking after her at home and she loved lavender and I frequently burned lavender candles for her.

The night she died I was sitting in my own livingroom and crying when I got the most beautiful smell of lavender. I felt she was letting me know that she was still with me and was OK.

I was in Leopardstown market some time after she died when I heard piped music. I didn't know where it was coming from and thought nothing of it until I heard 'Boulavogue.' This is the song my mother taught me the words of when I was four.

I think I got the message, don't you?

*How mad is that!*

Linda

# Doggy Style

About a year ago I was meeting my girlfriend's parents for the first time. We were to meet them for a meal on the Saturday night so on the Friday night I decided to get in a few beers, but overindulged and really suffered on Saturday morning.

My girlfriend's family live in Scotland and my girlfriend and me were living together. I woke up on Saturday morning and my girlfriend was gone. I didn't know where but she usually disappears off to do some shopping at the weekends.

I came up with the idea of dressing up in a dog costume that I bought on eBay and jumping into the dog pen we have out the back. I saw the car pulling back into the drive ran out into the back garden and jumped over the gate into the dog pen.

I was in the pen howling and barking whilst trying to lick my unmentionables when my girlfriend and her parents, who I've never met, walked out of the car.

I had already leapt on my girlfriend doing doggy things that dogs do and had failed to see her parents. They must have thought I was psycho.

*How mad is that!*
Dav

# Date With Destiny

MY Grandad died the same day, date and time as my granny . . . 22 years later.
*How mad is that!*

# Red Handed

LAST SUMMER MY wife, Lynn, was out walking with our son and spotted my work van outside a house. She noticed someone inside and went over to ask him if he could tell me that she was outside and wanted to see me. The chap said no problem and headed off in the direction of the front door. She

waited for about 20 minutes before giving up on me and went home. That evening

I arrived home to a very pissed off other half who complained that she was left standing like a lemon waiting for me for ages and that the man she spoke to agreed to call me out. However she didn't realise that the dude she was talking to had broken into my work van and was in the process of making off with expensive tools and CDs. Not only did she frighten him she introduced herself too.

*How mad is that!*
Derek Dunphy

# NEWSPAPER MADS...

## *Snake in the FirstClass!*

Passengers on an Iarnrod Eireann train got a shock when an escaped snake slithered through the carriages.

Commuters on the Dublin to Galway train jumped on seats and tables as the corn snake escaped from the box he was being transported in by a pet shop owner.

CIE said the snake was recaptured shortly afterwards.

# Gaelic Unathletic Association

New research shows that hurlers are the fattest of all sportsmen.

Hurlers, Gaelic footballers and League of Ireland soccer players were all put through their paces for the Tralee Institute of Technology study.

Soccer players were the skinniest, followed by Gaelic footballers. Hurlers were found to have 18.4% body fat.

# *Very Nod!*

M y car window was smashed but my €300 radio wasn't taken or my mobile phone, which was in between the seats – but my bobblehead dog was.

*How mad is that!*
Liam, Limerick

## NAKED AMBITION

I ran down Tipperary town with nothing on only a pair of runners for a bet and got followed by the guards.

*How mad is that!*
Shane, Tipperary

189

# OuT pAtIeNt

Ray, I was over in London a few years ago visiting my brother. We were walking past the Old Bailey when we saw this lunatic in a white hospital gown running with a drip stuck in his arm (you know the one you use when you walk round the hospital with wheels), and being chased by two cops.

*How mad is that!*
Seamus, Tipperary

# ALWAYS ON YOUR MIND

At the time my mate's granny was dying, my mate's younger sister sent her mam a text saying, 'Hope Nana is OK'. It turns out she sent this message at the exact time of death . . . bit morbid this . . . but the weird thing is that her mam never got the message until exactly a month later, on her granny's month's mind, and at the time of death . . .

*How mad is that!*
Rachel and Amy

# NEWSPAPER MADS...

## Cereal Offender

Breakfast cereal cartoons could be the next thing on the banned list.

The European Commission is planning to ban the Honey Monster, Tony the Tiger and Ronald McDonald because of politicians' fears about the effect food advertising has on childhood obesity.

## NEWSPAPER MADS...

# Puppy Love

A love motel for amorous dogs has opened in Brazil.

The doggy love motel features a heart-shaped mirror on the ceiling and a headboard resembling a doggy bone.

The owner of the Sao Paulo establishment said: 'I'm absolutely certain this is the first one for dogs in the world.'

# Tenor Change

THE DAY PRINCESS Diana was killed my wife and her friend were talking about it and her friend said what I can't understand is why was Pavarotti following them on a motorbike.

*How mad is that!*
Martin, Armagh

# Ring of Truth

AS IF HAVING a sewage treatment plant in a place called 'Ringsend' wasn't puntastic enough, Dublin City Council has just announced that it's to increase the capacity of the plant. By how much? One turd! That's what the spokesman said, I swear.

*How mad is that!*

Gar

## NEWSPAPER MADS...

# Chimney Stuck

A clueless burglar would have been better off using the door during an attempted robbery. The pub robbery was botched by the hapless thief when he got trapped at the end of a 6-metre vent and had to be rescued by six firemen.

He was trapped overnight after he climbed down the circular chute before getting stuck in a narrow junction below. He was dragged out by a rope the next day.

# NEWSPAPER MADS...

## Nine out of Ten Cats Prefer It

UCC Zoology student Anthony Dunne has discovered that Irish cats prefer a live dinner to tinned catfood. He has calculated that Ireland's eight million cats go through 300 million-plus birds, small mammals and even other pets each year.

# *Local Call*

I was on the phone to my mate 120 miles from home. I had to go to the window of the pub to get better reception. As we were talking my mate passed by the window. Neither of us knew where the other one was and assumed we were each back in Limerick 120 miles away.

*How mad is that?*

# Missing Mail

My grandaunt married an Englishman many years ago and moved to Canada. About 25 years later in their new home her husband was fitting a new bathroom mirror when he found some old newspapers behind the old mirror scrunched up to hold the fibreglass insulation in place. In this mess there was an envelope addressed to a gentleman who lived across the lake from my aunt in Ireland. No work had never been done to the bathroom as long as my grandaunt and uncle lived there, and the previous owners had done nothing to it either, and they had been there about ten years. No one knows how that envelope got there and the man who it was addressed to had no links to Canada at all.

*How mad is that!*

Paul Clarke

# *Smear Campaign*

I was at Witness three years ago. It was a scorcher of a day but it had been a really wet summer up to then, so the ground was covered in muck. My friend was getting burnt and had no sun cream, so he decided to spread muck all over his arms and legs to protect his skin. After a while everyone started noticing an awful smell. It turned out he had actually spread sloppy cow shite all over himself! And he was sharing a tent with seven people!

*How mad is that!*

Aoife Conry

# LeGgiNG iT

A few years back I was standing on a high bank with my mates watching the West Cork Rally when we decided to cross to the other side of the road. I was last to go and as I did they made a whistle sound, I panicked and jumped over a wall, and all everyone could see was my two legs in the air. I was caught on camera and got a loud clap.

*How mad is that!*

Tony, Cork

# LOST AT SEA

A few years I was living in Australia and went swimming in the sea forgetting to take my wallet out of my trunks. I went back to the beach about an hour later and realised my wallet was gone and thought it had been nicked.

I went to the police station but they said nothing had been handed in. They advised me to ring home to cancel my credit cards. I went to use a payphone but the one outside the station wasn't working so I headed off down the street to find another one.

I eventually found a phone that was working. At the moment I was ringing home a couple walked past, overheard my conversation with the bank and said they had found my wallet washed up on the beach. They were on their way to the police station to hand it in.

*How mad is that!*
Anthony, Dublin

# Here We Go Again

In 1977 my mam went into hospital in Cork to have my older brother Liam. She met up with a woman called Ann from Rylane while she was there.

Then in 1979 when my mam was in the same hospital having me – who should be in the bed beside her having her third child but the same Ann from Rylane. They have kept up contact since that second meeting and are now best friends.

*How mad is that!*
Aoife Power, Cork

## Who's That Weirdo?

A cousin of mine never realised that our single uncle actually was our uncle. She thought he was just a weird family friend that came to every reunion.

*How mad is that!*

# Ford Fiasco

The Ray D'Arcy Show
WINNER

MY UNCLE was driving across the city late one night after dropping his cousin home after visiting his mother. As he drove he came across a man in a wheelchair trying to push himself up onto the footpath but he wasn't quite managing enough propulsion to mount the path and kept rolling back onto the road. My uncle stopped his 1980 gold Ford Fiesta and offered to help the man. He said to the man in the wheelchair, 'I have a length of rope in the boot, I'll tie it around the back bumper and you take the other end.'

The fella in the wheelchair took the other end of the rope. So they proceeded through the city centre when my uncle trundles over some speed ramps.

The Fiesta took them with a judder but the next thing my uncle saw was the wheelchair, without the man, sailing over the front of the car followed by the occupant of course. My uncle screeched to a stop and had to lift the chap into the car and drive him to the hospital.

The real tragedy of the story was that the man, who hadn't the use of his legs, and who now had broken some ribs and an arm, was in training for the Paralympics at the time.

*How mad is that!*
Ciara Byrne

# Magic Numbers

I was heading out to work yesterday in the car when I passed a dark posh car registration 02 W 1. I know that the first car to be registered in the county is always the mayoral car so it always catches my attention. About 15 minutes further out the road to Dunmore East I passed another dark posh car – 04 W 1.

How mad is that! Not mad enough you'll probably say. Well on the way home yesterday coming through town in traffic I saw 02 W 2!
*How mad is that!*

# Lucky Strike

Some years ago my boyfriend brought his cousin home from San Francisco to Croagh Patrick to do the touristy thing. It was late in the afternoon but they still decided to climb.

On taking a break my boyfriend reached for his cigarettes only to find that they were gone – after falling out of his pocket on the climb. None too pleased they continued on and finally got to the top. It was pitch black at this stage and they started the descent almost immediately.

Half way down my boyfriend lost his footing and slipped on a steep part and slid a few yards down. To stop himself from going any further he stretched out his hands and managed to stop. He felt something under his hand once he stopped. What was it but his box of cigarettes with lighter in box intact!

*How mad is that!*

Sharon

# DrEaM lOVEr

When I was working in Dublin a few years ago I would return to the capital every Sunday evening while my friends would go on the beer around the town. I was very tired after travelling up from Limerick so I went to bed about 10pm. At about 12 midnight I woke up after having a dream about my friend (who was on the beer at the time). In the dream she was kissing a boy from the town. I had to ring her to tell her what I dreamed because she was mad about the boy. There was silence on the phone for a couple of seconds and then she told me she was just with him.

*How mad is that!*
Siobhan Hartnett

# Dead Funny

I am a paramedic in Derry and one night we were sent to the local psychiatric hospital for a cardiac arrest. Unfortunately the patient died and was left for the local undertaker to take care of. About an hour later we were again dispatched for a vehicle which had crashed through the barrier on the dual carriageway.

On arrival we discovered the undertaker's hearse lying in a ditch with a stretcher in the back but no deceased or driver in the vehicle. Suddenly around the corner comes a guy running just wearing a pair of trousers and covered in blood. I stopped him and asked him was he okay, he replied yes and stated that he was driving the hearse. It then emerged he was another patient from the hospital who had stolen the hearse for the craic and totally wrecked it.

*How mad is that!*
Bill Forbes

# GeTtinG A-rouNd

I went out on Saturday night and woke up on Sunday with a flag from a golf course in the bed next to me. I don't remember taking it.

*How mad is that!*

I just found out this morning that my girlfriend and me have been texting in to try and get a Bobblehead Ray for each other as a surprise.

*How mad is that!*

# Crossed Lines

I HAVE A mobile shop and an oul lad came in one day looking for the spray for a sick dog. I said I wouldn't have it and sent him to the local chemist. He then told me he was already there but they said they only had a big container of it and he only needed a small bit.

The Ray D'Arcy Show

WINNER

'Sure you might have some in the back. You could put it in a bottle for me,' he said.

I also had someone in looking for a wheelbarrow one day!

*How mad is that!*

James

# *Camping Gas*

Two summers ago me and a few friends went on a small camping trip to Kerry. We set up camp on some beach, then went out drinking that night and returned to the tents. That morning someone from the local community association informed us that we were no longer welcome on the beach. So for the rest of the day we walked around looking for our new site. We found a secluded little patch of land and decided to set up there that night. We went out again and returned to our tents that night. The next morning we were woken by a load of noise outside the tent. We got my friend to stick his head out the door of the tent. He pulled his head back and announced we were dead centre in the middle of a car boot sale, which was in full swing.

*How mad is that!*

Niall

# SpEaK oF tHe DeViL

When I was in college I watched one of Pearse Brosnan's James Bond films on a Wednesday night. I enjoyed it so much I watched another one on Friday night. The next night, back at home, we watched *The Thomas Crown Affair,* also starring Brosnan, on the TV. On Saturday morning I was working in the shop of a petrol/diesel garage when who should pull in for a refill in a flash Merc only Pearse Brosnan. I still have his autograph and picture.

*How mad is that!*
Colm, Tipperary

## NEWSPAPER MADS...

# Cursed Thieves

The mayor of the Austrian town of Fucking has pleaded with English speaking tourists to stop nicking the town's road signs.

Siegfried Hauppi says it's a big problem but it doesn't mean the townsfolk are going to change their name.

'We had a vote last year on whether to rename the town, but decided to keep it as it was.'

# NEWSPAPER MADS...

## *Word Jam*

An organisation to solve the traffic jam problems in our cities has a name longer than the average rush hour log jam.

The Multi Initiative for Rationalised Accessibility and Clean Liveable Environments (MIRACLES) met in Cork earlier this year.

## Sea of Love

Passers by called 999 after they heard screams from a rubber dinghy in Devon. The emergency services rushed to the scene to find a naked couple making love. One lifeboatman said, 'I've never seen such things in a two-metre inflatable at such an early hour.'

# KEEPING UP WITH THE JONES

I used to have an 02 Mitsubishi Pajero Sport in green. While out walking I noticed that a house nearby also had a 02 Mitsubishi Pajero in green outside. It was exactly the same as mine.

Last month I bought a new car – an 05 navy Mitsubishi Pajero Sport. Within a week I noticed that the same house also had an identical navy 05 Pajero Sport outside.

*How mad is that!*

Marc, Clare

# *Well Connected*

I've been going out with my boyfriend for three and a half years. Two weeks ago we discovered that he is actually my godmother's second cousin. My godmother is married to my uncle for over 20 years.

*How mad is that!*

Pamela

# COT NEXT?

When I was in college in England I was at a nightclub. I started chatting up this girl and it turns out we share the same birthday 3.10.73. It gets better – it turns out we were in cots next to each other in Castlebar hospital.

*How mad is that!*
Seanie, Sligo

# Dunnes Stores Girl

A girl I know was in Dunnes Stores not so long ago when she noticed a photograph lying face down on the floor. She picked up the photo only to discover the picture was of her when she was a child.

She brought the picture home and told her mother the story. It turns out that the picture had fallen from her aunt's purse earlier that day.

*How mad is that!*
Jennie Noons

# NEWSPAPER MADS...

## Spanker

An elderly man in Galway is urging bathers to spank him while he waves a walking stick at them

The old man expresses his wishes in notes he leaves on a beach. One note read, 'Don't be frightened ladies. If you want you can come and spank me.'

Stunned sun worshippers saw him remove his clothes and holler at the top of his voice.

## Garda Clean-up

Gardaí recently broke up a criminal gang involved with laundering of a different sort.

A washing powder theft operation was uncovered when a man was arrested when caught with €15,000 worth of household cleaning materials.

It is believed the cleaning products were being sold door to door.

# EaSY GOLFeR

I once played golf with Dennis Hopper and Stephen in the lashing rain in Wicklow. Denis had a shouting match with us, as he couldn't work out the difference between yards and metres for the course.

His assistant kept pulling out balls from his pocket and throwing them on the ground so that he could tell Dennis that's where the ball landed.

*How mad is that!*
Robert Trench

# Three's Company

My friend and I went to Oxegen last year. When we arrived at the car park we realised that three slabs of beer, a tent, two sleeping bags and three bags of clothes was far too much to carry by ourselves. My friend convinced three blokes from the North to carry our excess baggage.

We made a deal. Katie told the guys that she would 'reveal' herself if they would carry our bags. The guys lugged the bags for about a mile. When we got there my friend reneged on the deal but settled for a kiss. We didn't see the guys after that.

At this year's Oxegen just after we had got our tent set up and were strolling through the campsite we turned around to see the three blokes from the North from last year!

*How mad is that!*

Roy

# TrAVeLLinG cOMpAnioNs

I drive the 46A. On Friday a girl got on in town and got off at Foxrock. We smiled at each other. I raced to Dun Laoghaire and back to Donnybrook, got changed out of my uniform and ran out to get a bus into town, standing room only. Who's standing there but the same girl.

I got off in town then went to get a bus to Heuston Station. Who's at the stop? – the same girl! More smiles. I went for a coffee, got on the train, five minutes later who sits across from me – the same girl!

To top it off we both got off in Tullamore.

On Sunday night I got the train from Galway to Tullamore. I got on – and there she was again. We both freaked out and started chatting. She'd gone to Galway on the Saturday and I'd stayed in Tullamore.

*How mad is that!*

# *Hotpants*

I once sprayed my testicles with deep heat and then had to sit into a bath of cold water to cool them down.
*How mad is that!*

I once ate bananas with Roy Keane in the back of a vegetable van. Strange but true.
*How mad is that!*
Gav, Cork

# NEWSPAPER MADS...

## *Paddling the Internet*

A 99-year-old granny has just completed a computer course in Dublin.

The woman said she completed the computer course in her local library because, 'I heard my grandchildren mention they had booked holidays online or seen something on the Internet and it bugged me,' she said.

# Fowl Mouthed

A parrot in England is in solitary confinement after hurling abuse at visiting dignitaries. Barney the five-year-old macaw told the local mayor to 'f**k off' and then told the vicar: 'You can f**k off too.' His owner blamed late night television which Barney frequently watched.

# Feather Brains

Thieves in El Salvador took a parrot from a house they had robbed so there would be no clues. When the gang's getaway car was stopped by police in a routine check the parrot squawked, 'Robbery!'

The car was searched and the stolen goods found in the boot.

# NEWSPAPER MADS...

## The Law's an Ass

An out-of-touch English judge admitted during a recent case that he did not know what a sofa bed was. Judge Seddon Cripps asked a witness what he was talking about when reference was made to that type of furniture.

The judge asked: 'How can a bed be turned into a sofa?'

Earlier the 63-year-old judge said he didn't know what a futon was.

# A Roof Night

I was at a house party one night and got very drunk. I got word that the host's parents were on the way home so I decided to climb onto the roof of the house to watch what was happening and fell asleep. I woke up hours later soaking wet in the rain and all the lads were in the kitchen with the parents.

*How mad is that!*

# Old Hand

MY FRIEND GREG was sitting in his jeep on his own, stopped at traffic lights a couple of years ago, looking out the driver's window daydreaming. Suddenly the passenger door opened and an elderly lady jumped into the passenger seat and had buckled herself in before Greg could react. His obvious reaction was, 'What do you think you're doing?' to which she started to explain she had terrible arthritis and needed to get to the doctor for a prescription for painkillers. Her condition was so bad that she was unable to walk and was depending on Greg's good nature to drive her the rest of the way to the doctor's surgery.

With the lights turning green, and she being an old lady in pain, Greg agreed to drive her to the doctor. She started giving him directions on which route to take. When they reached Ballybricken at the top of Waterford, which was the wrong direction for him, there was a queue at a stop sign. At this point the old dear said this will do nicely, thanked Greg, hopped out of the jeep with no sign of painful arthritis, and happily skipped off into the pub. Thanks very much you sucker!

*How mad is that!*

Neil

# *Mistaken Identity*

I work for Standard Brands in County Louth. Every year on the 31st December I have to collect the auditor from the hotel and bring him or her to the factory for the annual stocktake at 8am. Last year the auditor was going to be a girl called Jennifer Murray, but as I had only spoken to her on the phone, I didn't know what she would look like.

I got to the Fairways Hotel at 7.50am and saw a girl standing in reception, arms folded, obviously waiting on somebody.

I parked the car (a Fiat Punto) and went back up to the doors. As I walked in she walked straight up to me. I said 'Jennifer' and she replied 'McCourt'. I nodded and she smiled and followed me to the car. We left the hotel and went back up the road towards the factory.

I decided to make small talk so I asked her how long she was doing accountancy as the auditors usually send a junior with one or two years experience. She told me she was fully qualified, ACCA like me, which seemed strange.

She then told me I had missed her turn off to which I said I know the factory as I work there. She then told me she was going to the Point Road and said that she was going to do a stock take.

She told me to stop and said, 'What kind of taxi is this – a Fiat Punto as a taxi!'

It turns out her name was Jennifer McCourt, an accountant who was waiting on a taxi in the hotel when I turned up. Realising I had picked up the wrong girl I took her back to the hotel, where a minibus with a big yellow taxi plate on top was waiting for her.

When I walked in, another girl walked straight up to me laughing her head off and said she was Jennifer Murray and she was wondering how long it would take me to come back for her as she was watching all along. This story has now gone around the auditor's office in Dublin and every year a new junior starts taking the piss.

*How mad is that!*
Denis McCourt

# Deep Heat Sleep

A FEW YEARS AGO I came home after a Saturday night out a little worse for wear and decided it was a bit too cold so I boiled the kettle and filled my hot water bottle and went to bed. The following morning I woke up all refreshed but for some reason a little bit sore so I lifted the duvet only to discover that I had slept through a scalding from the hot water bottle which went from my back down my thigh which I still have a visible scar from. The anaesthetic affect of alcohol!

*How mad is that!*
Shane, Kerry

# NEWSPAPER MADS...

## Fashion Police

An American state has announced that it is to make the wearing of low trousers that reveal underwear illegal.

Lawmakers in the State of Virginia aim to make the wearing of below-the-waist underwear in a 'lewd or indecent manner' an offence. Wearers face a $40 fine for their fashion statement.

## On the Pull-Over

An Irish survey shows that over 90% of men would stop to help a stranded female motorist change a wheel but 20% of them admitted that the lady's attractiveness would influence their decision.

# TONGUE TWISTER

I can turn my tongue into a number of shapes
– one being a flower and another a whale's
tongue.

*How mad is that!*
Eddie W

# NUTs

I smell like coconuts.

*How mad is that!*
Gimme a Bobblehead or else!

#  Cheeky

I don't want a Bobblehead, Ray.

*How feckin' mad is that?*